CONTENTS

WHAT CAN ASTROLOGY
do for me?

Astrology is a powerful tool for self-awareness. The idea that we are all connected—that the shifting energies of the Sun, Moon, and planets above affect us here on Earth—is an ancient and philosophical belief. Astrology isn't fortune-telling—it can't predict your future and it doesn't deal in absolutes. It simply says that you are part of the universe around you, and by studying the stars, it's possible to learn more about yourself.

Why is this so important? Because the better understanding you have of your own inner makeup—your skills, your talents, your needs, and your fears—the more insight you gain into why you act the way you do. And this gives you choices, empowering you to make changes and to build on your strengths. It makes it easier to feel confident and to accept yourself, quirks and all.

There are countless daily horoscopes in newspapers, magazines, and online. But this book looks at more than just your star sign, which is only a small part of your personality picture. It helps you to find your Rising sign, which was appearing over the Eastern horizon at the time of your birth, and has a lot to tell you about the way others see you. You can also work out your Moon sign, which reveals the real you deep down inside, giving you the chance to get to grips with your innermost emotions, desires, fears, and obsessions.

With a clearer picture of who you are, life becomes less complicated. Instead of trying to live up to others' expectations and being someone you're not, you can work instead on becoming the best version of yourself possible—someone who understands their talents and needs, who is perfectly unique, and is happy.

What is
ASTROLOGY?

The stars and planets have always inspired a sense of wonder. The ancient peoples of Babylonia, Persia, Egypt, Greece, and India were all fascinated by the cycles of the Moon, the rising and setting of the Sun, the position of the constellations, and what it all meant. As these civilizations developed, they connected what they saw in the sky with the people and events on Earth, and astrology was born.

In ancient times, astrology was used to help monarchs rule. Kings and emperors would employ astrologers to predict the weather, speak to the gods, and help manage the country.

Modern astrology has evolved to help ordinary people like you and me understand ourselves better—how we behave, how we feel about each other, and how we can make the best of who we are.

THE SIGNS OF THE ZODIAC

Today we know that the planets revolve around the Sun, but astrology is based on how we see the solar system from here on Earth. The Zodiac is a group of 12 constellations that, from our viewpoint, seem to rotate around Earth over the course of a year, like a huge wheel. These constellations are named for the animals and objects that our ancestors thought they looked most like—the ram, the lion, the scorpion, and so on. Your Sun sign tells you which of the constellations the Sun was moving through on the day you were born. The signs have a natural order that never varies, beginning with Aries. The dates given on the right change slightly from year to year for the same reasons we have a leap year—each of our days is slightly longer than 24 hours. If you were born at the beginning or end of a sign, called "the cusp," it's worth checking your Sun sign online to be sure.

ARIES March 21–April 20	**LIBRA** September 23–October 22
TAURUS April 21–May 21	**SCORPIO** October 23–November 21
GEMINI May 22–June 21	**SAGITTARIUS** November 22–December 21
CANCER June 22–July 22	**CAPRICORN** December 22–January 20
LEO July 23–August 23	**AQUARIUS** January 21–February 19
VIRGO August 24–September 22	**PISCES** February 20–March 20

THE FOUR ELEMENTS

*Each Sun sign is associated with one of four elements—
Fire, Earth, Air, and Water.*

FIRE

Aries, Leo, Sagittarius
Fire signs are passionate, dynamic, and temperamental.
They mix well with: Fire and Air types

EARTH

Taurus, Virgo, Capricorn
Earth signs are practical, cautious, and reliable.
They mix well with: Water and Earth types

AIR

Gemini, Libra, Aquarius
Air signs are quick, curious, and adventurous.
They mix well with: Air and Fire types

WATER

Cancer, Scorpio, Pisces
Water signs are sensitive, emotional, and kind.
They mix well with: Earth and Water types

THE PLANETS

Astrology looks at the positions of the stars and planets at the time and place of your birth. The Sun and Moon aren't technically planets, but they're referred to that way by astrologers for ease of use. The Sun is a great place to start—it's the most important object in the solar system. Your Sun sign describes the essence of your identity, and says a great deal about your potential—the person you might become.

The position the Moon held in the sky at the time of your birth has a strong influence, too. It describes your emotions—how you feel deep inside. It can give you a better understanding of what you need to feel loved and cared for.

And there's also your Rising sign. This is the sign of the Zodiac that was appearing over the Eastern horizon at the time of your birth. It tells you more about how you interact with the world around you, especially to new situations. It's the filter through which you perceive the world and the impression you give to others on first meeting. Which means it's also how others often see you.

The positions of the other planets—Venus, Mercury, Mars, etc.—in your birth chart all have their own effect. But these three taken together—Sun, Moon, and Rising sign—will give you a deeper understanding of who you are and what you could become, your strengths and weaknesses, your real self.

Your SUN sign

LEO

July 23–August 23

SYMBOL
The Lion

ELEMENT
Fire

RULING PLANET
Sun

BIRTHSTONE
Peridot

COLOR
Gold

BODY PART
Heart

DAY OF THE WEEK
Sunday

FLOWER
Sunflower

CHARACTER TRAITS
Loud, big-hearted, enthusiastic

KEY PHRASE
"I will"

YOUR SUN SIGN

When people talk about astrology and ask about your star sign, they're referring to your Sun sign. It tells you which of the 12 constellations of the Zodiac the Sun was moving through on the day you were born. This makes it easy to work out, which is one of the reasons for its popularity. If you'd like to know the Sun sign of a friend or family member, the table on page 7 shows which days the Sun occupies each of the signs over the course of a year.

The Sun is the heart of your chart—it's the essence of who you are and symbolizes the potential of what you can achieve. It's important to remember, though, that it is only a part of the whole picture when it comes to astrology. It's a wonderful starting point, but there are many other layers encasing your core identity, all of which affect the inner you.

ALL ABOUT YOU

Born with the Sun in Leo, you have the potential to shine a light on things, allowing others to discover hidden truths. Brimming with confidence and energy, you have a wonderful knack for making others feel good about themselves. Maybe that's because letting loose and enjoying a good time with friends is your favorite pastime—usually dressed to impress, you're the star of any party.

Luckily, this happy-go-lucky disposition doesn't mean you forget about the important stuff: you're also incredibly generous, not just with your money but with your love and loyalty, too.

Your closest friends already know this—and will enjoy basking in the glorious, sunny rays of your warm and welcoming personality.

Leos always want to be the center of attention: you positively buzz with drama and charisma. This means you'll often be first in line when it comes to auditions for school plays. But no one's "purr"-fect—even the king of the jungle. Pride can sometimes get the better of you and lead to misunderstandings in your close relationships, especially if you hang out with sensitive Water signs.

Likes

The spotlight
Any excuse to have fun
Looking magnificent
Giving compliments
Being the boss
Bright colors

Dislikes

Running out of cash
Going unnoticed
Keeping secrets

HOW TO BRING OUT YOUR BEST

"I am lion, hear me roar!" Although Leos are one of the Zodiac's bravest signs, that doesn't mean you are superhuman. If your unwavering loyalty and generosity isn't immediately returned, you can feel a bit bewildered. Your lesson? Not to take everything to heart: your friends simply don't possess the supreme strength and confidence that comes so naturally to you. And they might not understand that occasionally you need their support, too. Once they come to realize this, those friendships just get stronger.

You can sometimes take on too much, thinking that there's nothing you can't achieve. This is a wonderful attitude to have, but it does mean you can suddenly run out of steam. When that happens, take time to recharge—a catnap should top up your energy levels.

Strengths

Encouraging
Charming
Leader
Loyal
Generous
Optimistic

Weaknesses

Arrogant
Proud
Show-off

SECRET FEARS

Having to count the nickels and dimes makes you luxury-loving Leos seriously unhappy, so you will be creative when it comes to making money. This means you'll find ingenious ways to afford the things you want—whether that's running a lemonade stand in your front yard or running errands in your neighborhood. You're often quite the entrepreneur.

When you take a shine to someone, you'll circle your potential boyfriend or girlfriend until you're sure they're definitely the one for you. As a Fixed sign, you want to make sure any romance is for keeps before you hand over that huge heart of yours. Try to take a more relaxed approach to these relationships and have plenty of fun, too.

Most likely to . . .

Talk too loud
Look good even when feeling bad
Interrupt
Say, "I deserve this"
Splurge
Be the life and soul of the party
Put your best foot forward

Your RISING sign

YOUR RISING SIGN

Your Rising sign, also known as your Ascendant, is the sign that was rising over the Eastern horizon (the place where the Sun rises each day) when you were born. It describes how you see the world and the people around you and how they see you—the first impression that you give and receive, the image you project, and the initial reaction you might have to a new situation. A person with Leo Rising, for example, may strike you as warm and engaging, whereas Pisces Rising is more sensitive and possibly shy. Because the Ascendant is determined by the exact time and place you were born, it is the most personal point in your chart. Many astrologers believe this makes it just as important as your Sun sign.

HOW TO FIND YOUR ASCENDANT

This is where it gets a bit tricky. There's a reason that popular astrology only deals with your Sun sign—your Rising sign can be more difficult to work out. But don't be put off. If you know your Sun sign and your time of birth, you can use the table on the right to give you a good idea. To be totally accurate you do need to take into account factors like time zone and daylight savings, and there are plenty of free online calculators that will do just that.

YOUR SUN SIGN	YOUR HOUR OF BIRTH											
	6:00 AM to 8:00 AM	8:00 AM to 10:00 AM	10:00 AM to 12:00 PM	12:00 PM to 2:00 PM	2:00 PM to 4:00 PM	4:00 PM to 6:00 PM	6:00 PM to 8:00 PM	8:00 PM to 10:00 PM	10:00 PM to 12:00 AM	12:00 AM to 2:00 AM	2:00 AM to 4:00 AM	4:00 AM to 6:00 AM
ARIES ♈	♉	♊	♋	♌	♍	♎	♏	♐	♑	♒	♓	♈
TAURUS ♉	♊	♋	♌	♍	♎	♏	♐	♑	♒	♓	♈	♉
GEMINI ♊	♋	♌	♍	♎	♏	♐	♑	♒	♓	♈	♉	♊
CANCER ♋	♌	♍	♎	♏	♐	♑	♒	♓	♈	♉	♊	♋
LEO ♌	♍	♎	♏	♐	♑	♒	♓	♈	♉	♊	♋	♌
VIRGO ♍	♎	♏	♐	♑	♒	♓	♈	♉	♊	♋	♌	♍
LIBRA ♎	♏	♐	♑	♒	♓	♈	♉	♊	♋	♌	♍	♎
SCORPIO ♏	♐	♑	♒	♓	♈	♉	♊	♋	♌	♍	♎	♏
SAGITTARIUS ♐	♑	♒	♓	♈	♉	♊	♋	♌	♍	♎	♏	♐
CAPRICORN ♑	♒	♓	♈	♉	♊	♋	♌	♍	♎	♏	♐	♑
AQUARIUS ♒	♓	♈	♉	♊	♋	♌	♍	♎	♏	♐	♑	♒
PISCES ♓	♈	♉	♊	♋	♌	♍	♎	♏	♐	♑	♒	♓

WHAT YOUR RISING SIGN SAYS ABOUT YOU

Once you have figured out your Ascendant, you are ready to discover more about how you see the world, and how it sees you.

ARIES RISING

Action Aries adds rocket fuel to Leo's already dynamic personality. You always seem to have one foot out the door, rushing off to meet a friend or get involved in some new activity. Image is important to you, and you take time over the way you present yourself. Your courage and enthusiasm makes you popular, and once people get to know you, they soon discover your fun-loving heart. Try not to get too impatient with others: not everyone has your energy reserves.

TAURUS RISING

You have a fixed way of viewing the world, making you tough when you need to be, but also stubborn. Thoughtful, warm, and loyal, you are steadfast and purposeful, and once you start something, your ability to keep going is legendary. Your creative nature is offset perfectly by Taurus's practicality—you are capable not only of generating ideas but also carrying them out. Home comforts are important to you, and you need a relaxing environment in which to recharge.

GEMINI RISING

You're a real social butterfly. Part of your charm is that you make your friends feel completely at ease around you by being genuinely interested in what's going on in their lives. Occasionally this can border on nosiness, but your sunny energy means no one really minds how inquisitive you can be. Your strong desire to communicate your thoughts and ideas, coupled with your inner self-confidence, means you enjoy expressing yourself in front of others. Remember to take a step back now and then and let others have their time in the limelight.

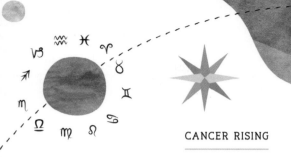

CANCER RISING

Leo's Fire is tempered by Cancer's Water element just enough to bring a sense of realism into your life. You instinctively know how to bring out the best in yourself, and this quiet confidence is picked up by your friends. Your ability to laugh at yourself is an attractive quality, and you have a strong desire to protect those who are less fortunate than you. Watch out for things that make you overly emotional; you can be easily hurt, especially when it comes to pride.

LEO RISING

Double Leo means your sunny outlook and stamina is impossible to ignore. The essence of your inner self matches the way you deal with others, making for a harmonious combination. You are gentle-hearted, although this can sometimes be overlooked thanks to your full-speed-ahead attitude. Thankfully, those closest to you know how generous and warm you truly are. Your theatricality means you thrive whenever you're put where you were born to be—center stage. Just be mindful not to get too wrapped up in your own hype.

VIRGO RISING

Virgo's practical nature can temper Leo's love of drama. You might be happy holding court at a party one moment, then craving some alone-time the next. And Virgo's serious side can mean you come across as less fun-loving than you really are. The good news is you're a stickler for detail and have real staying power once you've started a project. Just beware you don't get too caught up in making things perfect.

LIBRA RISING

Creative and artistic, you have an outer elegance that matches the beauty within. You care deeply about what others think of you, but there's no need to worry— your fair-mindedness and warm heart make you a hit in any friendship circle. You excel at teamwork and working in groups, especially when it wins you the appreciation of others. Your inner desire to be center stage is balanced by Libra's need for calm and harmony—a winning combination.

SCORPIO RISING

Powerful and intense, your fixed nature can mean you're a force to be reckoned with. Nothing fazes you, and when you've set your sights on something, you absolutely refuse to give up. Just be mindful of trampling others to get what you want. You crave the limelight, and people are drawn to your mysterious and magnetic charm, but your warm inner core is well hidden from all but those closest to you.

SAGITTARIUS RISING

A happy Fire combination, your sunny character matches your bright and breezy personality. Sociable and warm, you easily catch the eye of those around you, making friends with ease. A natural leader, your enthusiasm is catching, and you work well with others, offering support when it's needed. Your optimism and love of learning mean you are capable of realizing your hopes and dreams, whatever they may be—that Sagittarius free spirit that demands constant change is complemented by Leo's staying power.

CAPRICORN RISING

This combination can go one of two ways. On the one hand Capricorn's ambition combined with your inner confidence means little is out of your reach. But on the other, your need for praise and admiration mixed with Capricorn's determination to succeed can see you come across as arrogant and self-serving. From a young age, you surprise the adults in your life with your strong sense of responsibility. Your competitive streak can occasionally lead to trouble, so being genuinely happy about your friends' success is something to work on.

AQUARIUS RISING

Leos with Aquarius Rising are often concrete in their thinking—you have a tendency to see situations in terms of right or wrong and don't always consider the gray areas. However, you are a natural trailblazer, brimming with ideas and blessed with the energy required to make them happen. Clever and thoughtful, you see the bigger picture, and this keeps your tendency to be dramatic in check. Generous and imaginative in equal measure, when you choose to, you can bring out the best in anyone.

PISCES RISING

Pisces brings with it a humanitarian view of the world—your warm heart works well with Pisces' need to help others. If a friend is feeling blue, you'll be the one trying your best to cheer them up. Ironically, though, you're likely to resist help when it's the other way round. If you can let people in, even just a little, the rewards will be worth it. Your caring nature and readiness to forgive and forget means few people are as loved as you. This makes for a happy combination.

Your MOON sign

YOUR MOON SIGN

The Moon rules your emotions and your inner moods, telling you what you need to feel safe, comfortable, and loved. Knowing your Moon sign should give you a more complete picture of your unique self, helping you to express needs you might be struggling to understand. Suppose your Sun sign is Aries but being first has never been important to you—a Moon in Virgo may be telling you to hang back and fade into the background. Or you might have the Sun in home-loving Cancer but feel an urge to get out there and see the world. Perhaps that's because your Moon is in freedom-loving Sagittarius.

HOW TO FIND YOUR MOON SIGN

Just like your Rising sign, finding your Moon sign is more complicated than finding your Sun sign. That's because the Moon seems to move so quickly, taking just about a month to pass through all of the constellations. Thankfully, the tables on the right and on the next page make finding it a simple process.

First, find your year of birth. Then locate your birth month at the top of the table. Find your date of birth in the column below it, and this will give you your Moon sign. If your date of birth isn't listed, the one before it is your Moon sign.

For example, suppose your date of birth is March 4, 1995. The date before this is March 2, for which the Moon sign is Aries. This would mean your Moon sign is Aries.

	JAN	FEB	MAR	APR	MAY	JUN	JUL	AUG	SEP	OCT	NOV	DEC

BORN IN THE YEAR 1995

JAN	FEB	MAR	APR	MAY	JUN	JUL	AUG	SEP	OCT	NOV	DEC
2 Aqu	1 Pis	2 Ari	1 Tau	1 Gem	2 Leo	2 Vir	3 Sco	1 Sag	2 Aqu	1 Pis	3 Tau
4 Pis	3 Ari	5 Tau	3 Gem	3 Can	5 Vir	4 Lib	5 Sag	3 Cap	5 Pis	3 Ari	5 Gem
7 Ari	5 Tau	7 Gem	6 Can	6 Leo	7 Lib	6 Sco	7 Cap	5 Aqu	7 Ari	5 Tau	8 Can
9 Tau	8 Gem	10 Can	9 Leo	8 Vir	9 Sco	8 Sag	9 Aqu	7 Pis	9 Tau	8 Gem	10 Leo
12 Gem	10 Can	12 Leo	11 Vir	10 Lib	11 Sag	10 Cap	11 Pis	9 Ari	12 Gem	10 Can	13 Vir
14 Can	13 Leo	14 Vir	13 Lib	13 Sco	13 Cap	12 Aqu	13 Ari	12 Tau	14 Can	13 Leo	15 Lib
16 Leo	15 Vir	17 Lib	15 Sco	15 Sag	15 Aqu	14 Pis	15 Tau	14 Gem	17 Leo	15 Vir	17 Sco
19 Vir	17 Lib	19 Sco	17 Sag	17 Cap	17 Pis	17 Ari	18 Gem	17 Can	19 Vir	18 Lib	19 Sag
21 Lib	19 Sco	21 Sag	19 Cap	19 Aqu	19 Ari	19 Tau	20 Can	19 Leo	21 Lib	20 Sco	21 Cap
23 Sco	22 Sag	23 Cap	21 Aqu	21 Pis	21 Tau	22 Gem	23 Leo	22 Vir	23 Sco	22 Sag	23 Aqu
25 Sag	24 Cap	25 Aqu	24 Pis	23 Ari	24 Gem	24 Can	25 Vir	24 Lib	26 Sag	24 Cap	25 Pis
27 Cap	26 Aqu	27 Pis	26 Ari	26 Tau	27 Can	27 Leo	28 Lib	26 Sco	28 Cap	26 Aqu	28 Ari
30 Aqu	28 Pis	30 Ari	28 Tau	28 Gem	29 Leo	29 Vir	30 Sco	28 Sag	30 Aqu	28 Pis	30 Tau
				31 Can		31 Lib		30 Cap		30 Ari	

BORN IN THE YEAR 1996

JAN	FEB	MAR	APR	MAY	JUN	JUL	AUG	SEP	OCT	NOV	DEC
1 Gem	3 Leo	1 Leo	2 Lib	2 Sco	2 Cap	2 Aqu	2 Ari	1 Tau	3 Can	2 Leo	2 Vir
4 Can	5 Vir	3 Vir	4 Sco	4 Sag	4 Aqu	4 Pis	4 Tau	3 Gem	5 Leo	4 Vir	4 Lib
6 Leo	8 Lib	6 Lib	7 Sag	6 Cap	6 Pis	6 Ari	7 Gem	6 Can	8 Vir	7 Lib	6 Sco
9 Vir	10 Sco	8 Sco	9 Cap	8 Aqu	9 Ari	8 Tau	9 Can	8 Leo	10 Lib	9 Sco	9 Sag
11 Lib	12 Sag	10 Sag	11 Aqu	10 Pis	11 Tau	11 Gem	12 Leo	11 Vir	13 Sco	11 Sag	11 Cap
14 Sco	14 Cap	13 Cap	13 Pis	12 Ari	13 Gem	13 Can	14 Vir	13 Lib	15 Sag	13 Cap	13 Aqu
16 Sag	16 Aqu	15 Aqu	15 Ari	15 Tau	16 Can	16 Leo	17 Lib	15 Sco	17 Cap	16 Aqu	15 Pis
18 Cap	18 Pis	17 Pis	17 Tau	17 Gem	18 Leo	18 Vir	19 Sco	18 Sag	19 Aqu	18 Pis	17 Ari
20 Aqu	20 Ari	19 Ari	20 Gem	19 Can	21 Vir	21 Lib	21 Sag	20 Cap	21 Pis	20 Ari	19 Tau
22 Pis	23 Tau	21 Tau	22 Can	22 Leo	23 Lib	23 Sco	24 Cap	22 Aqu	23 Ari	22 Tau	22 Gem
24 Ari	25 Gem	23 Gem	25 Leo	25 Vir	26 Sco	25 Sag	26 Aqu	24 Pis	26 Tau	24 Gem	24 Can
26 Tau	27 Can	26 Can	27 Vir	27 Lib	28 Sag	27 Cap	28 Pis	26 Ari	28 Gem	27 Can	26 Leo
29 Gem		28 Leo	30 Lib	29 Sco	30 Cap	29 Aqu	30 Ari	28 Tau	30 Can	29 Leo	29 Vir
31 Can		31 Vir		31 Sag		31 Pis		30 Gem			31 Lib

BORN IN THE YEAR 1997

JAN	FEB	MAR	APR	MAY	JUN	JUL	AUG	SEP	OCT	NOV	DEC
3 Sco	1 Sag	1 Sag	1 Aqu	1 Pis	1 Tau	1 Gem	2 Leo	3 Lib	3 Sco	1 Sag	1 Cap
5 Sag	4 Cap	3 Cap	4 Pis	3 Ari	4 Gem	3 Can	4 Vir	6 Sco	5 Sag	4 Cap	3 Aqu
7 Cap	6 Aqu	5 Aqu	6 Ari	5 Tau	6 Can	5 Leo	7 Lib	8 Sag	8 Cap	6 Aqu	5 Pis
9 Aqu	8 Pis	7 Pis	8 Tau	7 Gem	8 Leo	8 Vir	9 Sco	10 Cap	10 Aqu	8 Pis	8 Ari
11 Pis	10 Ari	9 Ari	10 Gem	9 Can	11 Vir	10 Lib	12 Sag	12 Aqu	12 Pis	10 Ari	10 Tau
13 Ari	12 Tau	11 Tau	12 Can	12 Leo	13 Lib	13 Sco	14 Cap	15 Pis	14 Ari	12 Tau	12 Gem
15 Tau	14 Gem	13 Gem	14 Leo	14 Vir	16 Sco	15 Sag	16 Aqu	17 Ari	16 Tau	14 Gem	14 Can
18 Gem	16 Can	16 Can	17 Vir	17 Lib	18 Sag	18 Cap	18 Pis	19 Tau	18 Gem	17 Can	16 Leo
20 Can	19 Leo	18 Leo	19 Lib	19 Sco	20 Cap	20 Aqu	20 Ari	21 Gem	20 Can	19 Leo	19 Vir
23 Leo	21 Vir	21 Vir	22 Sco	22 Sag	22 Aqu	22 Pis	22 Tau	23 Can	23 Leo	21 Vir	21 Lib
25 Vir	24 Lib	23 Lib	24 Sag	24 Cap	24 Pis	24 Ari	24 Gem	25 Leo	25 Vir	24 Lib	24 Sco
28 Lib	26 Sco	26 Sco	27 Cap	26 Aqu	26 Ari	26 Tau	27 Can	28 Vir	28 Lib	26 Sco	26 Sag
30 Sco		28 Sag	29 Aqu	28 Pis	29 Tau	28 Gem	29 Leo	30 Lib	30 Sco	29 Sag	28 Cap
		30 Cap		30 Ari		30 Can	31 Vir				31 Aqu

BORN IN THE YEAR 1998

JAN	FEB	MAR	APR	MAY	JUN	JUL	AUG	SEP	OCT	NOV	DEC
2 Pis	2 Tau	2 Tau	2 Can	2 Leo	3 Lib	3 Sco	2 Sag	3 Aqu	2 Pis	1 Ari	2 Gem
4 Ari	4 Gem	4 Gem	4 Leo	4 Vir	5 Sco	5 Sag	4 Cap	5 Pis	4 Ari	3 Tau	4 Can
6 Tau	7 Can	6 Can	7 Vir	7 Lib	8 Sag	8 Cap	6 Aqu	7 Ari	6 Tau	5 Gem	6 Leo
8 Gem	9 Leo	8 Leo	9 Lib	9 Sco	10 Cap	10 Aqu	8 Pis	9 Tau	8 Gem	7 Can	9 Vir
10 Can	11 Vir	11 Vir	12 Sco	12 Sag	13 Aqu	12 Pis	11 Ari	11 Gem	10 Can	9 Leo	11 Lib
13 Leo	14 Lib	13 Lib	14 Sag	14 Cap	15 Pis	14 Ari	13 Tau	13 Can	13 Leo	11 Vir	14 Sco
15 Vir	16 Sco	16 Sco	17 Cap	16 Aqu	17 Ari	16 Tau	15 Gem	15 Leo	15 Vir	14 Lib	16 Sag
18 Lib	19 Sag	18 Sag	19 Aqu	19 Pis	19 Tau	18 Gem	17 Can	18 Vir	17 Lib	16 Sco	19 Cap
20 Sco	21 Cap	21 Cap	21 Pis	21 Ari	21 Gem	21 Can	19 Leo	20 Lib	20 Sco	19 Sag	21 Aqu
23 Sag	23 Aqu	23 Aqu	23 Ari	23 Tau	23 Can	23 Leo	22 Vir	23 Sco	22 Sag	21 Cap	23 Pis
25 Cap	25 Pis	25 Pis	25 Tau	25 Gem	25 Leo	25 Vir	24 Lib	25 Sag	25 Cap	24 Aqu	25 Ari
27 Aqu	27 Ari	27 Ari	27 Gem	27 Can	28 Vir	28 Lib	26 Sco	28 Cap	27 Aqu	26 Pis	28 Tau
29 Pis		29 Tau	29 Can	29 Leo	30 Lib	30 Sco	29 Sag	30 Aqu	30 Pis	28 Ari	30 Gem
31 Ari		31 Gem		31 Vir		31 Cap				30 Tau	

BORN IN THE YEAR 1999

JAN	FEB	MAR	APR	MAY	JUN	JUL	AUG	SEP	OCT	NOV	DEC
1 Can	1 Vir	1 Vir	2 Sco	2 Sag	3 Aqu	2 Pis	1 Ari	2 Gem	1 Can	1 Vir	1 Lib
3 Leo	4 Lib	3 Lib	4 Sag	4 Cap	5 Pis	5 Ari	3 Tau	4 Can	3 Leo	4 Lib	3 Sco
5 Vir	6 Sco	6 Sco	7 Cap	7 Aqu	8 Ari	7 Tau	5 Gem	6 Leo	5 Vir	6 Sco	6 Sag
7 Lib	9 Sag	8 Sag	9 Aqu	9 Pis	10 Tau	9 Gem	7 Can	8 Vir	8 Lib	9 Sag	8 Cap
10 Sco	11 Cap	11 Cap	12 Pis	11 Ari	12 Gem	11 Can	9 Leo	10 Lib	10 Sco	11 Cap	11 Aqu
12 Sag	14 Aqu	13 Aqu	14 Ari	13 Tau	14 Can	13 Leo	12 Vir	13 Sco	12 Sag	14 Aqu	13 Pis
15 Cap	16 Pis	15 Pis	16 Tau	15 Gem	16 Leo	15 Vir	14 Lib	15 Sag	15 Cap	16 Pis	16 Ari
17 Aqu	18 Ari	17 Ari	18 Gem	17 Can	18 Vir	17 Lib	16 Sco	18 Cap	17 Aqu	18 Ari	18 Tau
19 Pis	20 Tau	19 Tau	20 Can	19 Leo	20 Lib	20 Sco	19 Sag	20 Aqu	20 Pis	21 Tau	20 Gem
22 Ari	22 Gem	21 Gem	22 Leo	21 Vir	23 Sco	22 Sag	21 Cap	22 Pis	22 Ari	23 Gem	22 Can
24 Tau	24 Can	23 Can	24 Vir	24 Lib	25 Sag	25 Cap	24 Aqu	24 Ari	24 Tau	25 Can	24 Leo
26 Gem	26 Leo	26 Leo	27 Lib	26 Sco	28 Cap	27 Aqu	26 Pis	27 Tau	26 Gem	27 Leo	26 Vir
28 Can		28 Vir	29 Sco	28 Sag	30 Aqu	30 Pis	28 Ari	29 Gem	28 Can	29 Vir	28 Lib
30 Leo		30 Lib		31 Cap			30 Tau		30 Leo		31 Sco

BORN IN THE YEAR 2000

JAN	FEB	MAR	APR	MAY	JUN	JUL	AUG	SEP	OCT	NOV	DEC
3 Sag	1 Cap	2 Aqu	1 Pis	3 Tau	1 Gem	2 Leo	1 Vir	2 Sco	1 Sag	3 Aqu	2 Pis
5 Cap	4 Aqu	4 Pis	3 Ari	5 Gem	3 Can	4 Vir	3 Lib	4 Sag	4 Cap	5 Pis	5 Ari
7 Aqu	6 Pis	7 Ari	5 Tau	7 Can	5 Leo	7 Lib	5 Sco	6 Cap	6 Aqu	8 Ari	7 Tau
10 Pis	8 Ari	9 Tau	7 Gem	9 Leo	7 Vir	9 Sco	8 Sag	9 Aqu	9 Pis	10 Tau	9 Gem
12 Ari	11 Tau	11 Gem	9 Can	11 Vir	9 Lib	12 Sag	10 Cap	11 Pis	11 Ari	12 Gem	11 Can
14 Tau	13 Gem	13 Can	11 Leo	13 Lib	12 Sco	14 Cap	13 Aqu	14 Ari	13 Tau	14 Can	13 Leo
16 Gem	15 Can	15 Leo	14 Vir	15 Sco	14 Sag	16 Aqu	15 Pis	16 Tau	16 Gem	16 Leo	15 Vir
18 Can	17 Leo	17 Vir	16 Lib	18 Sag	17 Cap	19 Pis	18 Ari	18 Gem	18 Can	18 Vir	18 Lib
20 Leo	19 Vir	20 Lib	18 Sco	20 Cap	19 Aqu	21 Ari	20 Tau	20 Can	20 Leo	20 Lib	20 Sco
23 Vir	21 Lib	22 Sco	21 Sag	23 Aqu	22 Pis	24 Tau	22 Gem	23 Leo	22 Vir	23 Sco	22 Sag
25 Lib	23 Sco	24 Sag	23 Cap	25 Pis	24 Ari	26 Gem	24 Can	25 Vir	24 Lib	25 Sag	25 Cap
27 Sco	26 Sag	27 Cap	26 Aqu	28 Ari	26 Tau	28 Can	26 Leo	27 Lib	26 Sco	27 Cap	27 Aqu
29 Sag	28 Cap	29 Aqu	28 Pis	30 Tau	28 Gem	30 Leo	28 Vir	29 Sco	29 Sag	30 Aqu	30 Pis
			30 Ari		30 Can		30 Lib		31 Cap		

BORN IN THE YEAR 2001

JAN	FEB	MAR	APR	MAY	JUN	JUL	AUG	SEP	OCT	NOV	DEC
1 Ari	2 Gem	1 Gem	2 Leo	1 Vir	2 Sco	1 Sag	3 Agu	1 Pis	1 Ari	2 Gem	2 Can
4 Tau	4 Can	4 Can	4 Vir	3 Lib	4 Sag	4 Cap	5 Pis	4 Ari	4 Tau	4 Can	4 Leo
6 Gem	6 Leo	6 Leo	6 Lib	6 Sco	7 Cap	6 Aqu	8 Ari	6 Tau	6 Gem	7 Leo	6 Vir
8 Can	8 Vir	8 Vir	8 Sco	8 Sag	9 Aqu	9 Pis	10 Tau	9 Gem	8 Can	9 Vir	8 Lib
10 Leo	10 Lib	10 Lib	10 Sag	10 Cap	11 Pis	11 Ari	12 Gem	11 Can	10 Leo	11 Lib	10 Sco
12 Vir	12 Sco	12 Sco	13 Cap	13 Aqu	14 Ari	14 Tau	15 Can	13 Leo	13 Vir	13 Sco	12 Sag
14 Lib	15 Sag	14 Sag	15 Aqu	15 Pis	16 Tau	16 Gem	17 Leo	15 Vir	15 Lib	15 Sag	15 Cap
16 Sco	17 Cap	16 Cap	18 Pis	18 Ari	19 Gem	18 Can	19 Vir	17 Lib	17 Sco	17 Cap	17 Aqu
18 Sag	20 Agu	19 Aqu	20 Ari	20 Tau	21 Can	20 Leo	21 Lib	19 Sco	19 Sag	20 Aqu	20 Pis
21 Cap	22 Pis	22 Pis	23 Tau	22 Gem	23 Leo	22 Vir	23 Sco	21 Sag	21 Cap	22 Pis	22 Ari
23 Aqu	25 Ari	24 Ari	25 Gem	24 Can	25 Vir	24 Lib	25 Sag	24 Cap	23 Aqu	25 Ari	25 Tau
26 Pis	27 Tau	26 Tau	27 Can	27 Leo	27 Lib	26 Sco	28 Cap	26 Aqu	26 Pis	27 Tau	27 Gem
28 Ari		29 Gem	29 Leo	29 Vir	29 Sco	29 Sag	30 Aqu	29 Pis	28 Ari	30 Gem	29 Can
31 Tau		31 Can		31 Lib		31 Cap			31 Tau		31 Leo

BORN IN THE YEAR 2002

JAN	FEB	MAR	APR	MAY	JUN	JUL	AUG	SEP	OCT	NOV	DEC
2 Vir	1 Lib	2 Sco	1 Sag	2 Aqu	1 Pis	1 Ari	2 Gem	1 Can	1 Leo	1 Lib	1 Sco
4 Lib	3 Sco	4 Sag	3 Cap	5 Pis	4 Ari	4 Tau	5 Can	3 Leo	3 Vir	3 Sco	3 Sag
6 Sco	5 Sag	6 Cap	5 Aqu	7 Ari	6 Tau	6 Gem	7 Leo	5 Vir	5 Lib	5 Sag	5 Cap
9 Sag	7 Cap	9 Aqu	8 Pis	10 Tau	9 Gem	8 Can	9 Vir	7 Lib	7 Sco	7 Cap	7 Aqu
11 Cap	10 Aqu	11 Pis	10 Ari	12 Gem	11 Can	11 Leo	11 Lib	9 Sco	9 Sag	9 Aqu	9 Pis
13 Aqu	12 Pis	14 Ari	13 Tau	15 Can	13 Leo	13 Vir	13 Sco	12 Sag	11 Cap	12 Pis	12 Ari
16 Pis	15 Ari	16 Tau	15 Gem	17 Leo	15 Vir	15 Lib	15 Sag	14 Cap	13 Aqu	14 Ari	14 Tau
18 Ari	17 Tau	19 Gem	18 Can	19 Vir	17 Lib	17 Sco	18 Cap	16 Aqu	16 Pis	17 Tau	17 Gem
21 Tau	20 Gem	21 Can	20 Leo	21 Lib	20 Sco	19 Sag	20 Aqu	19 Pis	18 Ari	20 Gem	19 Can
23 Gem	22 Can	24 Leo	22 Vir	23 Sco	22 Sag	21 Cap	22 Pis	21 Ari	21 Tau	22 Can	22 Leo
26 Can	24 Leo	26 Vir	24 Lib	25 Sag	24 Cap	24 Aqu	25 Ari	24 Tau	23 Gem	24 Leo	24 Vir
28 Leo	26 Vir	28 Lib	26 Sco	28 Cap	26 Aqu	26 Pis	27 Tau	26 Gem	26 Can	27 Vir	26 Lib
30 Vir	28 Lib	30 Sco	28 Sag	30 Aqu	29 Pis	28 Ari	30 Gem	29 Can	28 Leo	29 Lib	28 Sco
			30 Cap			31 Tau			30 Vir		30 Sag

JAN	FEB	MAR	APR	MAY	JUN	JUL	AUG	SEP	OCT	NOV	DEC

BORN IN THE YEAR 2003

JAN	FEB	MAR	APR	MAY	JUN	JUL	AUG	SEP	OCT	NOV	DEC
1 Cap	2 Pis	1 Pis	3 Tau	2 Gem	1 Can	1 Leo	2 Lib	2 Sag	1 Cap	2 Pis	2 Ari
3 Aqu	5 Ari	4 Ari	5 Gem	5 Can	4 Leo	3 Vir	4 Sco	4 Cap	4 Aqu	5 Ari	4 Tau
6 Pis	7 Tau	6 Tau	8 Can	7 Leo	6 Vir	5 Lib	6 Sag	6 Aqu	6 Pis	7 Tau	7 Gem
8 Ari	10 Gem	9 Gem	10 Leo	10 Vir	8 Lib	7 Sco	8 Cap	9 Pis	8 Ari	10 Gem	9 Can
11 Tau	12 Can	11 Can	12 Vir	12 Lib	10 Sco	9 Sag	10 Aqu	11 Ari	11 Tau	12 Can	12 Leo
13 Gem	14 Leo	14 Leo	14 Lib	14 Sco	12 Sag	12 Cap	12 Pis	13 Tau	13 Gem	15 Leo	14 Vir
16 Can	16 Vir	16 Vir	16 Sco	16 Sag	14 Cap	14 Aqu	15 Ari	16 Gem	16 Can	17 Vir	16 Lib
18 Leo	18 Lib	18 Lib	18 Sag	18 Cap	16 Aqu	16 Pis	17 Tau	18 Can	18 Leo	19 Lib	19 Sco
20 Vir	21 Sco	20 Sco	20 Cap	20 Aqu	19 Pis	18 Ari	20 Gem	21 Leo	21 Vir	21 Sco	21 Sag
22 Lib	23 Sag	22 Sag	23 Aqu	22 Pis	21 Ari	21 Tau	22 Can	23 Vir	23 Lib	23 Sag	23 Cap
24 Sco	25 Cap	24 Cap	25 Pis	25 Ari	23 Tau	23 Gem	24 Leo	25 Lib	25 Sco	25 Cap	25 Aqu
26 Sag	27 Aqu	26 Aqu	27 Ari	27 Tau	26 Gem	26 Can	27 Vir	27 Sco	27 Sag	27 Aqu	27 Pis
29 Cap		29 Pis	30 Tau	30 Gem	28 Can	28 Leo	29 Lib	29 Sag	29 Cap	29 Pis	29 Ari
31 Aqu		31 Ari				30 Vir	31 Sco		31 Aqu		

BORN IN THE YEAR 2004

JAN	FEB	MAR	APR	MAY	JUN	JUL	AUG	SEP	OCT	NOV	DEC
1 Tau	2 Can	3 Leo	1 Vir	1 Lib	2 Sag	1 Cap	1 Pis	2 Tau	2 Gem	1 Can	1 Leo
3 Gem	4 Leo	5 Vir	4 Lib	3 Sco	4 Cap	3 Aqu	4 Ari	5 Gem	5 Can	3 Leo	3 Vir
6 Can	7 Vir	7 Lib	6 Sco	5 Sag	6 Aqu	5 Pis	6 Tau	7 Can	7 Leo	6 Vir	6 Lib
8 Leo	9 Lib	9 Sco	9 Sag	7 Cap	8 Pis	7 Ari	8 Gem	10 Leo	10 Vir	8 Lib	8 Sco
10 Vir	11 Sco	12 Sag	11 Cap	9 Aqu	10 Ari	10 Tau	11 Can	12 Vir	12 Lib	10 Sco	10 Sag
13 Lib	13 Sag	14 Cap	12 Aqu	11 Pis	12 Tau	12 Gem	13 Leo	14 Lib	14 Sco	13 Sag	12 Cap
15 Sco	15 Cap	16 Aqu	14 Pis	14 Ari	15 Gem	15 Can	16 Vir	17 Sco	16 Sag	15 Cap	14 Aqu
17 Sag	17 Aqu	18 Pis	16 Ari	16 Tau	17 Can	17 Leo	18 Lib	19 Sag	18 Cap	17 Aqu	16 Pis
19 Cap	20 Pis	20 Ari	19 Tau	19 Gem	20 Leo	20 Vir	20 Sco	21 Cap	20 Aqu	19 Pis	18 Ari
21 Aqu	22 Ari	23 Tau	21 Gem	21 Can	22 Vir	22 Lib	23 Sag	23 Aqu	23 Pis	21 Ari	21 Tau
23 Pis	24 Tau	25 Gem	24 Can	24 Leo	25 Lib	24 Sco	25 Cap	25 Pis	25 Ari	23 Tau	23 Gem
25 Ari	27 Gem	28 Can	26 Leo	26 Vir	27 Sco	26 Sag	27 Aqu	27 Ari	27 Tau	26 Gem	25 Can
28 Tau	29 Can	30 Leo	29 Vir	28 Lib	29 Sag	28 Cap	29 Pis	30 Tau	29 Gem	28 Can	28 Leo
30 Gem				31 Sco		30 Aqu	31 Ari				31 Vir

BORN IN THE YEAR 2005

JAN	FEB	MAR	APR	MAY	JUN	JUL	AUG	SEP	OCT	NOV	DEC
2 Lib	1 Sco	2 Sag	3 Aqu	2 Pis	3 Tau	2 Gem	1 Can	2 Vir	2 Lib	1 Sco	2 Cap
4 Sco	3 Sag	4 Cap	5 Pis	4 Ari	5 Gem	5 Can	3 Leo	5 Lib	5 Sco	3 Sag	4 Aqu
6 Sag	5 Cap	6 Aqu	7 Ari	6 Tau	7 Can	7 Leo	6 Vir	7 Sco	7 Sag	5 Cap	7 Pis
8 Cap	7 Aqu	8 Pis	9 Tau	9 Gem	10 Leo	10 Vir	8 Lib	9 Sag	9 Cap	7 Aqu	9 Ari
10 Aqu	9 Pis	10 Ari	11 Gem	11 Can	12 Vir	12 Lib	11 Sco	12 Cap	11 Aqu	9 Pis	11 Tau
12 Pis	11 Ari	13 Tau	14 Can	14 Leo	15 Lib	15 Sco	13 Sag	14 Aqu	13 Pis	11 Ari	13 Gem
15 Ari	13 Tau	15 Gem	16 Leo	16 Vir	17 Sco	17 Sag	15 Cap	16 Pis	15 Ari	14 Tau	15 Can
17 Tau	16 Gem	17 Can	19 Vir	18 Lib	19 Sag	19 Cap	17 Aqu	18 Ari	17 Tau	16 Gem	18 Leo
19 Gem	18 Can	20 Leo	21 Lib	21 Sco	21 Cap	21 Aqu	19 Pis	20 Tau	19 Gem	18 Can	20 Vir
22 Can	21 Leo	22 Vir	23 Sco	23 Sag	23 Aqu	23 Pis	21 Ari	22 Gem	22 Can	21 Leo	23 Lib
24 Leo	23 Vir	25 Lib	26 Sag	25 Cap	25 Pis	25 Ari	23 Tau	24 Can	24 Leo	23 Vir	25 Sco
27 Vir	25 Lib	27 Sco	28 Cap	27 Aqu	28 Ari	27 Tau	26 Gem	27 Leo	27 Vir	26 Lib	28 Sag
29 Lib	28 Sco	29 Sag	30 Aqu	29 Pis	30 Tau	29 Gem	28 Can	29 Vir	29 Lib	28 Sco	30 Cap
		31 Cap		31 Ari			31 Leo			30 Sag	

BORN IN THE YEAR 2006

JAN	FEB	MAR	APR	MAY	JUN	JUL	AUG	SEP	OCT	NOV	DEC
1 Aqu	1 Ari	1 Ari	1 Gem	1 Can	2 Vir	2 Lib	1 Sco	2 Cap	1 Aqu	2 Ari	1 Tau
3 Pis	3 Tau	3 Tau	4 Can	3 Leo	5 Lib	5 Sco	3 Sag	4 Aqu	4 Pis	4 Tau	3 Gem
5 Ari	6 Gem	5 Gem	6 Leo	6 Vir	7 Sco	7 Sag	6 Cap	6 Pis	6 Ari	6 Gem	6 Can
7 Tau	8 Can	7 Can	9 Vir	8 Lib	10 Sag	9 Cap	8 Aqu	8 Ari	8 Tau	8 Can	8 Leo
9 Gem	10 Leo	10 Leo	11 Lib	11 Sco	12 Cap	11 Aqu	10 Pis	10 Tau	10 Gem	10 Leo	10 Vir
12 Can	13 Vir	12 Vir	14 Sco	13 Sag	14 Aqu	13 Pis	12 Ari	12 Gem	12 Can	13 Vir	13 Lib
14 Leo	16 Lib	15 Lib	16 Sag	16 Cap	16 Pis	15 Ari	14 Tau	15 Can	14 Leo	15 Lib	15 Sco
17 Vir	18 Sco	17 Sco	18 Cap	18 Aqu	18 Ari	17 Tau	16 Gem	17 Leo	17 Vir	18 Sco	18 Sag
19 Lib	20 Sag	20 Sag	20 Aqu	20 Pis	20 Tau	20 Gem	18 Can	19 Vir	19 Lib	20 Sag	20 Cap
22 Sco	23 Cap	22 Cap	22 Pis	22 Ari	22 Gem	22 Can	21 Leo	22 Lib	22 Sco	23 Cap	22 Aqu
24 Sag	25 Aqu	24 Aqu	25 Ari	24 Tau	25 Can	24 Leo	23 Vir	24 Sco	24 Sag	25 Aqu	24 Pis
26 Cap	27 Pis	26 Pis	27 Tau	26 Gem	27 Leo	27 Vir	26 Lib	27 Sag	26 Cap	27 Pis	27 Ari
28 Aqu		28 Ari	29 Gem	28 Can	29 Vir	29 Lib	28 Sco	29 Cap	29 Aqu	29 Ari	29 Tau
30 Pis		30 Tau		31 Leo			31 Sag		31 Pis		31 Gem

WHAT YOUR MOON SIGN SAYS ABOUT YOU

Now that you know your Moon sign, read on to learn more about your emotional nature and your basic inner needs.

MOON IN ARIES

You have an emotional need to be first. And you want to be first *now*—there's no time to waste. Brimming with enthusiasm and energy, you love to keep busy and find waiting difficult. Remember to open up and talk to those closest to you about your feelings—they can help you to slow down and deal with any difficult emotions as they arise.

MOON IN TAURUS

You love to be surrounded by beautiful possessions and enjoy food and clothes that make you feel good—you have a need for comfort. Familiarity and routine are important to you, and you don't deal well with sudden change. That stubborn streak means you're able to stand up for yourself and protect your own interests, just remember to relax once in a while and try new things.

MOON IN GEMINI

Self-expression is one of your driving forces with this mix. Talking, drawing, writing—you simply have to communicate your feelings. And you love to listen to other peoples' ideas, too. To feed your curious intellect, you've probably got a tower of books and magazines at your bedside. Just don't forget to exercise your body as well as your mind.

MOON IN CANCER

You were born to nurture others—whether that's through baking them a cake or being at the end of the phone when they need your reassuring words. Family is hugely important to you, and you want to feel loved and secure. Being honest about this and accepting your wonderfully sensitive and emotional nature will help you find inner peace.

MOON IN LEO

You have an emotional need to be admired—all you really want is for everyone to love you. Your kind heart and generosity toward your friends and family means you are usually surrounded by others, and the attention you crave is easily won. When things don't go your way, you have a tendency to be dramatic—don't let your pride stop you from asking for help when you need it.

MOON IN VIRGO

You are a gentle soul and appreciate the simple things in life. Helping others in small ways makes you feel needed, secure, and purposeful. A clean and tidy environment is a must, and everything has to be in its proper place. Learning not to fuss when something isn't perfect is a challenge—look for useful ways to keep your practical nature busy and happiness will follow.

MOON IN LIBRA

Close bonds are everything to you—you find strength and stability in your relationships with others. Your need for balance and harmony means you are an excellent peacemaker, skilled at helping people to see and understand another's perspective. Remember to feed your love of beauty with regular trips to art galleries and picturesque places.

MOON IN SCORPIO

Deep and emotionally intense, you need to trust those close to you with your innermost thoughts and desires. All or nothing, you have incredible intuition and can see right to the heart of people. Finding one or two close friends who you can really open up to and be honest with about your feelings is important for your happiness. When this happens, your inner strength is unmatched.

MOON IN SAGITTARIUS

Your need for freedom and space is overwhelming, but when you achieve it, you are bright, breezy, and filled with a zest for life. Always on the lookout for new things to try and people to meet, your energy and enthusiasm lifts the spirits of those around you. Planning is not your strong suit; you prefer to go with the flow and see where it takes you—preferably somewhere fun and interesting!

MOON IN CAPRICORN

Ambitious and practical, you want to work hard and achieve results. You are conscientious and naturally organized, with a clear picture of what you want and how you intend to get there. Remember to take time to kick back and relax—the strong front you present to those around you can hide your more sensitive side. Letting go occasionally isn't a sign of weakness.

MOON IN AQUARIUS

Your desire to be unique and unusual is powerful, and you need the space and freedom to be yourself. Emotionally detached, you are happily independent and have an ability to see the bigger picture. Try not to lose touch with those closest to you—life is full of ups and downs, and friends and family can offer valuable support through tougher times.

MOON IN PISCES

Dreamy and intuitive, your sensitive nature is highly attuned to the feelings of others. Be careful to steer clear of negative people—you're likely to absorb their vibes, and they will bring you down. It's important you learn how to take care of yourself when you feel overwhelmed emotionally. Escaping into a good book or listening to your favorite music can be a great way to reset.

ELEMENTS

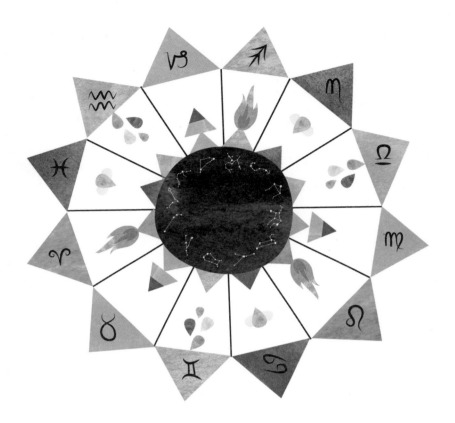

YOUR ELEMENTAL TYPE

Fire, Earth, Air, Water—in ancient times these were thought to contain everything that existed on Earth. Today that's no longer the case, but there's no denying their powerful effect on people's lives. Think of the heat from the Sun, the way earth is used to grow food, the water you consume, the air that you breathe. And like so much in astrology, each element has two sides. You drink water and rain helps plants to grow, but the force of a tsunami can wreak havoc and destruction. You have all four elements within you, but one or more of them will stand out. You could be a single type, or a mix of two or three. Your elemental type says a lot about you and those you interact with. When you meet someone you feel naturally comfortable with, it's often because you are elementally compatible.

IN YOUR ELEMENT

A warmhearted Fire sign, you are bold and boast a flair for the dramatic. Leo's confidence is hard to resist, and when you set your mind to something you're likely to achieve it. Unlike Aries, your flame is more stable—similar to a candle it burns slowly and steadily. This means you are happy to accept the status quo. Although it can also mean you have a tendency to be stubborn.

 FIRE WITH FIRE

You get along well with other Fire signs, just as Earth will with Earth, and so on. Relationships are led by the heart rather than by the head, as you both love others freely and with your whole being. When arguments arise, sparks can fly. Cool off with a walk or some kind of physical activity.

 FIRE WITH EARTH

Not ideally compatible, as Earth extinguishes fire, while "scorched Earth" is sterile and unproductive. Still, Earth can slow you down, acting as a grounding force, while you might get them going, energizing them with your passion and intensity. Finding a balance between stability and some form of newness and excitement is essential to a happy relationship.

 FIRE WITH AIR

Fire and Air signs are wonderfully compatible—think of oxygen to a flame. Air is full of ideas, and you are ready to put them into action. Together, you are a powerful, unstoppable force of activity. Remember, though, that relationships can become overwhelming if boundaries aren't put in place—air has the ability to fuel fire, but it can also blow it out.

 FIRE WITH WATER

Not an ideal mix. Fire and Water can be beautiful together, adventurous and dynamic, but if one is too dominant it can dampen Fire's energy or scorch Water's emotions. When it works, Water will bring sensitivity and comfort, while you provide motivation and the courage to act.

THE MISSING PIECE

How dominant Fire is within you depends on the influence of the other elements in your chart—ideally all four would be represented. Sometimes a lack of a particular element can cause an imbalance, making you feel rundown or stressed. The best way to counteract this is to tune in to the missing element and reharmonize yourself. Try the simple exercise below to get back in touch with any elements you're missing.

1. First, take a look at the Zodiac signs and their elements.

Fire: Aries, Leo, Sagittarius

Earth: Taurus, Virgo, Capricorn

Air: Gemini, Libra, Aquarius

Water: Cancer, Scorpio, Pisces

2. Now circle Fire, as this is the element that represents your Sun sign. You're certain to have some of this element. Then do the same for your Moon sign and your Ascendant, circling the element associated with each.

3. Looking at the list, there should be one or more elements you haven't circled.

Earth—a lack of Earth can make you feel disorganized, off-balance, or like you couldn't care less. You might want more routine, structure, or to stay focused.

Air—Air will help you to communicate better, feel more sociable, and lift your spirits. Use it to boost your curiosity and sharpen your wits.

Water—with Water missing you may struggle to get in touch with your emotions or worry you're being insensitive. You're looking to express yourself, to feel more creative and inspired.

4. Choose the element you would like to tune in to, whichever one you feel might benefit you. Then pick one of the ideas from the lists below. If Earth is missing, you could take a picnic to the park and sit on the grass. If it's Water, you could try a soak in the tub. You can use this exercise whenever you feel out of balance.

EARTH

Grow tomatoes
Pick wildflowers
Collect stones
Camp in the garden
Do cartwheels on the grass
Build a sandcastle
Roll down a hill

AIR

Fly a kite
Watch clouds go by
Blow bubbles
Feel the breeze
Breathe deep
Play with a balloon
Chase butterflies

WATER

Spend a day at the beach
Splash in a puddle
Sit by a fountain
Walk in the rain
Catch a wave
Snorkel

We are
FAMILY

WE'RE ALL IN THIS TOGETHER

When so much in your life is changing, your relationships with your parents can become even more important. If you're lucky, you get along well with yours, but even the most harmonious relationships can come under strain during the teenage years. How can astrology help? It can remind you that parents are people, too. They might not get everything right, but hopefully you believe that they have your best interests at heart. Learning more about who they are, why they do things, and how you relate to them can make it easier for all of you to move forward together.

MOTHER MOON

The Moon sign you are born with can tell you a lot about how you see and treat your mother. This is because your Moon sign represents your emotional needs—what you need to feel safe and secure—and these are most often fulfilled by your mother. How you react to her can make a big difference to the way she behaves around you. If you are visibly upset by certain things she does, she is likely to change her behavior the next time around. If you react with happiness and delight, she is more likely to repeat them.

Here's how you see your mother according to your Moon sign . . .

ARIES

You view your mother as strong, honest, and forthright. Sometimes, especially when she doesn't agree with your plans, this can make you feel as though she's taking over. Try not to push back too strongly, and remember she has your interests at heart.

TAURUS

You like to feel your mother is looking after all of your everyday needs and is dependable and reliable. Don't judge her too harshly if she doesn't always live up to your expectations—providing for others is often a careful balancing act, and she is likely doing her best.

GEMINI

Flighty and impulsive, you need your mother to give you the freedom to be yourself and make your own mistakes. Space and independence often have to be earned, though—what could you do to show her you're capable and trustworthy?

CANCER

Your longing for your mother's emotional attention can give you a wonderful bond and connection. However, the slightest hint of rejection from her can wound you deeply. Try not to take her reactions personally—it's okay for her to make choices and have goals that differ from yours.

LEO

You want to enjoy an open, honest relationship with your mother, where both of you say what you mean. Underlying this candor is a need for assurance and acceptance—when you feel vulnerable, be brave and explain to her how you feel.

VIRGO

You are aware of who gives what in your emotional relationship with your mother, and occasionally this can make you feel that she isn't there for you. Viewing her actions as "different" rather than "wrong" will help you to trust she is doing what she thinks is right.

LIBRA

You need your mother to recognize your emotional needs as valid and important. Try not to spend too much time putting others first—your relationship will flourish when you both accept the roles you play.

SCORPIO

You want your mother to respect your emotional boundaries and allow you alone-time when you need it. The trust between you can be intense and unconditional, so much so you may have to remind her to step back occasionally.

SAGITTARIUS

Upbeat and curious, your relationship works best when your mother is inspiring and encouraging, giving you the emotional freedom you need to expand your horizons. It's fine to chase independence, as long as you respect your mother's desire to give you roots.

CAPRICORN

You empathize strongly with your mother's feelings, so when she's struggling this can make you feel it's your fault. Learn to let go of this guilt—it's unintentional, and unhelpful. Instead, recognize how much you need each other's emotional support and encouragement.

AQUARIUS

You're not sure your mother's attempts to guide you are always necessary, and don't like to burden her with your problems. Asking for help and talking things through might be more useful than you imagine and can bring you closer together at the same time.

PISCES

Your mother's high expectations have made you stronger emotionally, even though there are times when you just want to feel like a child and let her take care of everything. Taking responsibility can be tough; don't be afraid to speak up when you need support.

HOW YOU SEE YOUR FATHER

Just as your Moon sign gives you an indication of how you see your mother, or whoever plays that nurturing role in your life, your Sun sign can reveal the way you view your father, or the caregiver who is most involved with discipline. Your relationship with this person is built over time. For girls, it can have a strong bearing on how you view any future romantic relationships, whereas boys will either rebel or identify with these traits.

With your Sun sign in Leo, you feel the warmth of your father's pride in you. He celebrates all of your successes and shares the news with anyone who will listen. Though he can be larger than life—he's the center of attention everywhere he goes—there's always room for you.

Now read on to find out how your father's Sun sign affects your relationship . . .

Your father's Sun sign will play a significant part in how you relate to him, and it can help you to understand why he acts the way he does— however infuriating it may sometimes seem!

ARIES

Your sisters and brothers rarely need to watch TV with you two around. Your sparky relationship—both of you are strong-willed—can be entertainment enough. You both need to learn when to pull back and keep things on the bright side.

TAURUS

Misunderstandings may arise if your reserved dad tries to talk you out of following a dream of stardom. He might think it's "showing off," but for you it's just how you are. Give him time to come round to the idea.

GEMINI

There's pride in this dynamic. In a way, you have similar outlooks—both signs tend to be eager to get out there and take on the world. You're also sociable folk and often enjoy mingling at all-age get-togethers.

CANCER

Your theatrical approach to life—dancing up the street, for example—might leave your father scratching his head in bewilderment. But your confidence tends to be infectious and, in time, some of it may even rub off on him.

LEO

With two Leos in the room, it can be a case of who roars loudest gets heard. You are so alike it can be hard to take a step back. But if you can manage it, a wonderfully magical relationship awaits.

VIRGO

There's often a deep devotion and respect between the two of you that other families can only dream about. Your Leonine showiness rarely fazes your father—in fact, he often appreciates it and knows where to come for free entertainment.

LIBRA

Your father loves your super-strong personality. In many ways he lives through those he's closest to, thriving on the differences in his own character. This means your relationship is close and harmonious; you know he has your back and you feel loved and understood.

SCORPIO

Life can be a rollercoaster with you two in town. You are unapologetically dramatic, and your dad isn't always averse to the spotlight either. This just leaves the rest of your family to pull up their seats and watch the entertainment unfold.

SAGITTARIUS

This is a fine pairing because you complement each other so well. Your playful nature encourages your dad's mischievous side. You probably enjoy setting up elaborate pranks—and see the funny side when you're on the receiving end.

CAPRICORN

Capricorn's sometimes serious nature can be softened by your bubbly attitude. It will help if you work with this energy throughout life, especially when you hit bumpy patches. Humor is often the secret to your lasting success.

AQUARIUS

The heat of your Leonine personality can warm the cool nature of your Aquarian father, but often the relationship is more one-sided, and you worship him from afar. Your shared love of travel could bring you closer together.

PISCES

Although you are at opposites of the spectrum—Leo can sometimes be self-centered while Pisces puts everyone else first—you balance each other out. It helps that you both have a rich imagination and understand each other's desire for success.

Best of
FRIENDS

FRIENDS FOR LIFE

Friends play an essential role in your happiness. They can help you to move forward when times are tough, see things from a new perspective, and encourage you just to have fun. Every good friend you make has different qualities that will influence you and allow you to make more of your potential. A friend might show you it can be better to hold back when all you want to do is rush in, motivate you to stick with that project right to the end, or inspire you to see an obstacle as a challenge. And astrology can be a great way to highlight those characteristics you're looking for in a friend. It can also tell you more about the type of friend you make for others.

WHAT KIND OF FRIEND ARE YOU?

Outgoing, confident, and full of energy, you don't have any problem making friends. You thrive on social occasions and love to be the life of a party, making people laugh and gaining their admiration. You're good at bringing people together, so you have a large circle of friends, but you also enjoy one-on-one time with those closest to you—as long as it doesn't interfere with other plans.

Strengths: *Honest, brave, positive*
Weaknesses: *Arrogant, self-centered, proud*
Friendship style: *Supportive, cheerful, humorous*

IF YOUR BEST FRIEND IS . . .

ARIES

Aries make friends easily. They're willing to help you achieve your goals, they see the best in you, and they're happy to take risks for you, too. They love to be someone's best friend and can find it difficult to feel second to anyone else. They are always on the lookout for new, super-fun adventures and are happy to take you along for the ride. They have a knack of bringing people from all walks of life together.

Strengths: *Loyal, generous, fun-loving*
Weaknesses: *Insensitive, demanding, petulant*
Friendship style: *Busy, fun, warm*

TAURUS

Considerate and charming, Taurus friends often have a talent for giving good advice. They like to take their time and allow friendships to develop slowly, but once you become close they treat you as a member of their family. As an Earth sign, they are dependable and grounded, and they make wonderful lifelong friends. Bear in mind they can place too much importance on material possessions, even judging others based on their wealth.

Strengths: *Caring, faithful, trustworthy*
Weaknesses: *Judgmental, stubborn, materialistic*
Friendship style: *Helpful, sweet, self-assured*

GEMINI

You'll need lots of energy to keep up with a Gemini friend. They love to have fun, do crazy things, and always have a story to tell. They'll make you laugh, but they can sometimes get a little carried away, perhaps exaggerating tales of their adventures in their effort to entertain you. They can be a bit gossipy, but they're not malicious. They're good listeners and will make you feel great, giving you lots of compliments—and always genuine ones, too.

Strengths: *Intelligent, energetic, fearless*
Weaknesses: *Impatient, easily bored, gossipy*
Friendship style: *Good listener, witty, spontaneous*

CANCER

Once you form a close connection with Cancer, you have a friend who has your back. They're considerate and like nothing better than to make you feel happy. Watch out though; they're deeply emotional, which means that if you argue—even over something small—you'll have to work hard to patch things up again.

Strengths: *Loving, caring, intuitive*
Weaknesses: *Unforgiving, anxious, sensitive*
Friendship style: *Warm, affectionate, protective*

VIRGO

With a Virgo by your side you'll always have somewhere to go when times are tough. They'll be there for you, giving you well-thought-out advice and a gentle sympathetic ear. Even when there's not a crisis, they're charming and kind. They like to be organized, so if they make plans, make sure you stick to them. They won't let you down, but they'll expect the same from you in return.

Strengths: *Warm, modest, smart*
Weaknesses: *Shy, serious, overly critical*
Friendship style: *Fixer, good communicator, reliable*

LIBRA

You can rely on your Libra friend to tell you how it is. They have a refreshing honesty, but they also have a diplomatic way of sparing your feelings. They love spending time with you and like nothing better than a chat (especially if they're the one doing the talking!). They can always see both sides, so if there's a disagreement it won't be for long.

Strengths: *Diplomatic, honest, sociable*
Weaknesses: *Indecisive, people pleaser, chatterbox*
Friendship style: *Laid-back, devoted, forgiving*

SCORPIO

It's an honor to be a Scorpio's best friend. They're selective, so they don't always have many, but the friendships they do make will be really special. Once you've cemented your friendship, they'll open their inner circle to you and will want to spend lots of time together. In return, they'll expect 100 percent loyalty and might not take it well if you let them down, so tread carefully.

Strengths: *Passionate, hospitable, perceptive*
Weaknesses: *Guarded, jealous, suspicious*
Friendship style: *Intense, selective, loyal*

SAGITTARIUS

Sagittarius are low-maintenance friends. Easygoing, positive, and happy-go-lucky, they're up for anything. If you fancy an adventure, give them a call, but don't expect too much of them feelings-wise. Their friendship circle is wide and diverse, so you'll get to meet lots of interesting people, but they are easily bored and can struggle with emotional closeness. On the plus side, they won't put too many demands on you, so give them some space and enjoy the ride.

Strengths: *Adventurous, positive, open-minded*
Weaknesses: *Impatient, insensitive, easily bored*
Friendship style: *Generous, undemanding, never dull*

CAPRICORN

You might have to put in some groundwork, but once you've cracked the seemingly aloof exterior of a Capricorn, you'll have yourself a genuine, warm, loving, and faithful friend. They'll show you complete devotion, through the good times and the bad. They're thoughtful and sensible and will know when to call it a night, but they will often surprise you with their sly sense of humor. They love to make you smile.

Strengths: *Responsible, supportive, faithful*
Weaknesses: *Condescending, standoffish, serious*
Friendship style: *Thoughtful, rational, work hard/play hard*

AQUARIUS

You'll have to share your Aquarius best friend—they'll probably flit in and out of lots of other friendships, too—but rest assured they've got your back and will go to the ends of the earth for you. They'll bring plenty of excitement and fun into your world, but they also treasure their alone-time, so don't put too many demands on them. They'll never pass judgment on you, no matter what you do.

Strengths: *Tolerant, independent, energetic*
Weaknesses: *Easily bored, rebellious, forgetful*
Friendship style: *Fun, exciting, unpredictable*

PISCES

A Pisces friend is a great listener who is sympathetic and caring and will always make time for you. They're the perfect friend if you need a shoulder to cry on, but they can sometimes get too emotionally involved. If there is any discord in your friendship, they are quick to blame themselves. Reassure them and let them know it's not their fault and you'll soon win back their love and support.

Strengths: *Loving, caring, good listener*
Weaknesses: *Sensitive, self-pitying, insecure*
Friendship style: *Supportive, sympathetic, selfless*

Your BIRTHDAY log

List the birthdays of your family and friends and discover their Sun signs

ARIES

March 21–April 20

Passionate, energetic, impulsive

....
....
....
....
....
....
....
....
....
....
....
....
....
....
....
....
....
....
....
....
....
....
....

TAURUS

April 21–May 21

Steady, tenacious, trustworthy

GEMINI

May 22–June 21

Intelligent, outgoing, witty

....
....
....
....
....
....
....
....
....
....
....
....
....
....
....
....
....
....
....
....
....
....

CANCER

June 22–July 22

Caring, home-loving, affectionate

LEO

July 23–August 23

Loud, big-hearted, fun

VIRGO

August 24–September 22

Organized, modest, responsible

LIBRA

September 23–October 22

Charming, creative, graceful

SCORPIO

October 23–November 21

Powerful, mysterious, magnetic

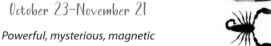

....
....
....
....
....
....
....
....
....
....
....
....
....
....
....
....
....
....
....
....
....
....
....
....

SAGITTARIUS

November 22–December 21

Adventurous, optimistic, lucky

CAPRICORN

December 22–January 20

Ambitious, dedicated, serious

AQUARIUS

Eccentric, independent, imaginative

PISCES

Dreamy, sensitive, compassionate

Lucky in
LOVE

WHY OPPOSITES REALLY DO ATTRACT

The sign opposite your Ascendant (your Rising sign) on your birth chart reveals who you will attract, and who will attract you. Known as your Descendant, it's the constellation that was setting on the Western horizon at the moment and place you were born.

This sign is everything you are not—a kind of mirror image, or two sides of the same coin.

Yet, strangely, you are often drawn to the qualities of this sign over and over again in the people you meet. It's possible that these characteristics are ones you feel you lack yourself, and you sense that the other person can fill in what's missing. Sometimes it really is true that opposites attract!

Ascendant	Descendant
Aries	Libra
Taurus	Scorpio
Gemini	Sagittarius
Cancer	Capricorn
Leo	Aquarius
Virgo	Pisces
Libra	Aries
Scorpio	Taurus
Sagittarius	Gemini
Capricorn	Cancer
Aquarius	Leo
Pisces	Virgo

WHAT DO YOU LOOK FOR?

Once you've matched up your Ascendant with your Descendant from the list on page 81, you can get to know the qualities that are most likely to attract you. You can use this information whether you're thinking about romance or friendship.

LIBRA DESCENDANT

You're looking for balance and harmony in your relationship, with someone who makes you feel interesting and important. You want to be listened to and value the ability to compromise. Gentleness and sensitivity are the qualities you're searching for.

SCORPIO DESCENDANT

You want an intense, passionate relationship with someone who will welcome you wholeheartedly into their world and want to spend lots of time with you. You are attracted to someone who will take control, but who will also look out for you and protect you.

SAGITTARIUS DESCENDANT

Adventure and fun are what you crave when it comes to love. You want someone open-minded who will accept you for who you are. You need to be given plenty of space to breathe and not be stifled by too many demands.

CAPRICORN DESCENDANT

You seek total dedication and devotion from those you love. You're happy to take your time and let a relationship develop naturally and aren't put off by someone who appears cool or guarded. You like an irreverent sense of humor, too.

AQUARIUS DESCENDANT

You are attracted to someone who is independent and has a full life outside of your relationship, although you want to know that if push comes to shove, they will be right there for you. You like to be kept on your toes.

PISCES DESCENDANT

You're not afraid of a deep relationship with someone who wears their heart on their sleeve. You want to be cared for, emotionally supported, and loved unconditionally. You want to be the center of someone's world.

ARIES DESCENDANT

You like someone to spar with and who lets you have your own way, but is still strong enough to put their foot down when the gravity of the situation demands it. You will need to respect your partner's strength, bravery, and integrity.

TAURUS DESCENDANT

Stability and reliability are high on your list of priorities when it comes to forming relationships. You dislike chaos and are drawn to people who you know won't surprise or disappoint you. Instead you want a partnership that's grounded and safe.

GEMINI DESCENDANT

You're attracted to someone who is spontaneous and fearless, and who can keep you entertained. You're likely to fall for someone who makes you feel super-special and is quick to recognize your achievements and boost your confidence.

CANCER DESCENDANT

You seek relationships where you're made to feel like one of the family, where your every need and demand is met, particularly emotionally. You want to feel warm and fuzzy and protected by those you love.

LEO DESCENDANT

You're drawn to someone who is strong, confident, and outgoing with a busy social life but who can also give you warmth and passion when required. You're attracted to those who can make you laugh and sweep you off your feet.

VIRGO DESCENDANT

You long for kindness and tenderness in a partnership, along with reliability. You want someone who can bring order into your life and who will think things through in a methodical way. Nothing should be left to chance.

Life at
SCHOOL

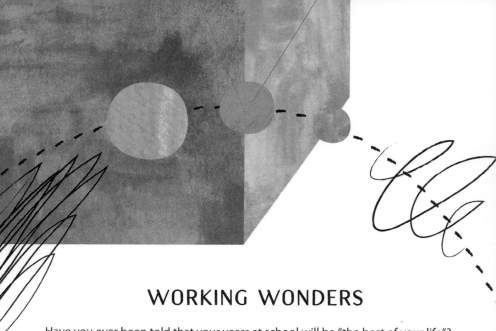

WORKING WONDERS

Have you ever been told that your years at school will be "the best of your life"? Do you think they will be? Why? Many different things will determine how much you enjoy your school days. And there are sure to be ups and downs along the way. But there are a couple of important factors that astrology can help with. The first is determining your skills and strengths, and the second is learning to work well with others. Identifying your natural interests and abilities can help you to develop a sense of purpose, and it's this that is most likely to motivate you to work hard and actually have fun while you do it. To have a sense of purpose, you need to know yourself and what it is you want from your life. Not what others want for you, or what is expected of you, but what actually makes you come alive.

HIDDEN TALENTS

Not all of your attributes will be immediately obvious. Just because you're a Leo doesn't mean you always feel generous, for example. You can think about what a typical Leo might be good at, but you are unique, and the stars are only a guide. Think about your strengths—both emotional and physical. The examples on the right may strike a chord with you, or you might want to create your own list.

BECAUSE YOU'RE . . . OUTGOING

You are talkative and extroverted, and enjoy large groups. You can think on your feet and like to make quick decisions. You usually act first and think later.

Maybe you could be a . . .

salesperson, marketing manager, community organizer

BECAUSE YOU'RE . . . ENERGETIC

You are a doer more than a thinker and take action to make things happen. Getting things done quickly and efficiently is more important to you than doing something perfectly. You love to achieve things, have bundles of energy, and work very hard.

Maybe you could be a . . .

lawyer, event manager, personal trainer

BECAUSE YOU'RE . . . CREATIVE

You're full of ideas. You love to work imaginatively with ideas or designs and are good at coming up with new ways to do things.

Maybe you could be a . . .

actor, performer, hairdresser, business developer

BECAUSE YOU'RE . . . DETERMINED

You enjoy completing tasks and persevere to finish what you started. You work hard to reach your goals and keep going even when things aren't working out.

Maybe you could be a . . .
police officer, realtor, cardiologist

BECAUSE YOU'RE . . . A LEADER

You love to spend your time persuading other people to do something, buy something, or believe in your cause. You're great at influencing and motivating others.

Maybe you could be a . . .
fundraiser, explorer, engineer, entrepreneur

FAMOUS LEO PEOPLE

Madonna—*Pop singer*
Amelia Earhart—*Aviation pioneer and author*
Daniel Radcliffe—*Actor*
Alfred Hitchcock—*Movie director and producer*
Megan Markle—*Actor, activist, and Duchess of Sussex*
J.K. Rowling—*Author*
Barack Obama—*Former US President*
Jennifer Lawrence—*Actor*

TEAM WORK

Working together with others is essential for almost any career path you choose to follow in later life. School can be competitive, yet working in collaboration with your peers rather than against them builds skills that today's employers are looking for.

Here's how well you work together with . . .

ARIES

There won't be any time wasted on getting a task done with you two around. It'll be full speed all the way, as long as you acknowledge differing opinions and occasionally agree to disagree. Get the balance right, and this team will go far, and with plenty of laughter, too.

TAURUS

Provided Taurus can keep up with you, or at least pretend to, you'll work well together on any task, especially if it's a practical one. You both need to be appreciated, but while you often crave glory and admiration, the bull simply wants credit where it's due. Try to share the limelight once in a while.

GEMINI

You have a mutual admiration that helps make this partnership click and, should any differences arise, you both possess a natural charm that will help smooth things over. Carve out specific roles for each other so you don't tread on each other's toes and things will move along nicely.

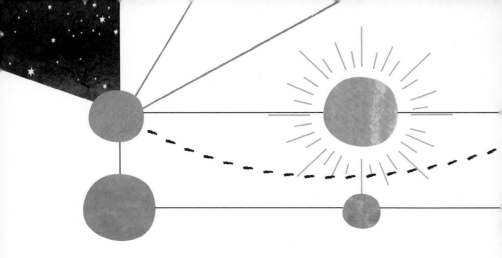

CANCER

While your Cancer colleague is still thinking things through, you've probably gone ahead and done it your way! Perhaps it's time to slow down, quiet that roar, and let this sensitive crab come out of its shell. You might even learn something.

LEO

With two such strong personalities coming together, there are bound to be a few shake-ups along the way, but if you can take turns and allow the other one to shine, the two of you can be a force to be reckoned with. Communication—particularly the listening part—is key if you want to achieve your full team potential.

VIRGO

If managed well, this unlikely pairing can be successful. It's all about appreciating each other's strong points and applying them appropriately. Simply put, Leo needs to be prepared to apply the brakes and give Virgo time to perfect things, and Virgo needs to let imperfections go in order not to cramp Leo's style. Go on, give it a try.

LIBRA

You two bring out the best in each other. You're both creative, sociable, popular, and fun-loving, but not to the detriment of your hard work and determination, which you have in droves. You enjoy each other's company, which is a great foundation for any team, and you make it fun for everyone else, too.

SCORPIO

This can be a battle of wills at times, with both sides craving attention and recognition, but if you want to succeed, you'll have to put your egos to one side. Ultimately you both want the same thing—to be the very best—so settle your disagreements and focus on the wider objective. It'll be easier that way.

SAGITTARIUS

When you two Fire signs combine your charms, there's no stopping you. You're both blessed with a natural energy and drive and, when you're members of the same team, you'll feed off each other with remarkable results. You're so well matched, you're hard to beat.

CAPRICORN

You two might never be the best of friends—you're just too different—but in the workplace you'll find a way of getting along. Capricorn needs to let you do your thing (even if it makes them uncomfortable), and you need to understand that boundaries don't necessarily mean cages.

AQUARIUS

You two can learn a lot from each other so that, as time goes on, your partnership will go from strength to strength. Leo can benefit from Aquarius' wider vision while Aquarius can pick up some of Leo's people skills. Get this right, and it's a match made in heaven.

PISCES

There needs to be some compromise on both sides for this to work, but it can be a winning combination. Deep down you both desire success and harmony, plus Pisces is warmed by your sunny personality, and you thrive on their unconditional adoration.

STERLING CHILDREN'S BOOKS
New York

An Imprint of Sterling Publishing Co., Inc.
1166 Avenue of the Americas
New York, NY 10036

ISBN 978-1-4549-3959-7

Distributed in Canada by Sterling Publishing Co., Inc.
c/o Canadian Manda Group, 664 Annette Street
Toronto, Ontario M6S 2C8, Canada

For information about custom editions, special sales, and premium and corporate
purchases, please contact Sterling Special Sales at 800-805-5489
or specialsales@sterlingpublishing.com.

Manufactured in China
Lot #:
2 4 6 8 10 9 7 5 3 1
08/19

sterlingpublishing.com

Design by Jo Chapman
Illustrations by Sara Thielker